How Great Thou Art

Carl Gustav Boberg (1885)

O Lord my God,

When I in awesome

wonder.

Consider all the worlds

Thy Hands have made.

I see the stars,

I hear the rolling

thunder.

Thy power throughout

the universe displayed.

It Is Well

Horacio Spafford (1873)

When peace like a river,

attendeth my way

When sorrows like sea

billows roll

Whatever my lot,

Thou hast taught me to know

It is well, it is well,

with my soul.

Amazing Grace
John Newton (1779)

Amazing Grace,

how sweet the sound

That saved a wretch

like me

I once was lost

but now am found

Was blind,

but now, I see.

Holy, Holy, Holy

Reginald Heiber (1826)

Holy, holy, holy!

Lord God Almighty!

Early in the morning

our song shall rise to thee

Holy, holy, holy!

Merciful and mighty

God in three persons,

blessed Trinity!

Praise To the Lord, The Almighty

Joachim Neander (1665)

Praise to the Lord, the Almighty,

the King of creation!

O my soul, praise Him,

for He is thy health and salvation!

All ye who hear,

now to His temple draw near

Sing now in glad adoration!

Great Is Thy Faithfulness

Thomas Chisholm (1923)

Great is Thy faithfulness

O God my Father

There is no shadow

Of turning with Thee

Thou changest not,

Thy compassions, they fail not

As Thou hast been

Thou forever wilt be.

Be Thou My Vision

Dallán Forgaill (6th Century)

Be Thou my vision,

O Lord of my heart

Naught be all else to me,

save that Thou art

Thou my best thought,

by day or by night

Waking or sleeping,

Thy presence my light.

All Creatures of Our God and King

St. Francis (1225)

All creatures of our God

and King

Lift up your voice

and with us sing

Alleluia! Alleluia!…Praise,

praise the Father,

praise the Son

And praise the Spirit,

Three in One!

All Hail The Power of Jesus' Name

Edward Perronet (1779)

All hail the power of Jesus' name!

Let angels prostrate fall

Bring forth the royal diadem

And crown him Lord of all.

To God Be the Glory

Fanny Crosby (1872)

To God be the glory,

great things He hath done

So loved He the world

that He gave us His Son

Who yielded His life

our redemption to win

And opened the life-gate

that all may go in.

When I survey The Wondrous Cross

Isaac Watts (1707)

When I survey

the wondrous cross

On which

the Prince of glory died

My richest gain

I count but loss

And pour contempt

on all my pride.

A Mighty Fortress Is Our God

Martin Luther (1529)

A mighty fortress is our God,

a bulwark never failing

Our helper He, amid the flood of mortal

ills prevailing

For still our ancient foe

doth seek to work us woe

His craft and power are great,

and, armed with cruel hate,

On earth is not his equal.

How Firm a Foundation

John Rippon (1787)

How firm a foundation,

ye saints of the Lord

Is laid for your faith

in His excellent Word!

What more can He say

than to you He hath said

Who unto the Savior

for refuge have fled?

Crown Him With Many Crowns

Matthew Bridges (1852)

Crown Him with many crowns,

the Lamb upon His throne

Hark! How the heavenly

anthem drowns

all music but its own

Awake, my soul, and sing of Him

who died for thee

and hail Him as thy matchless King

through all eternity.

Blessed Assurance

Fanny Crosby (1873)

Blessed assurance,
Jesus is mine!
Oh, what a foretaste
of glory divine!
Heir of salvation,
purchase of God
Born of His Spirit,
washed in His blood.

Jesus Paid it All

Elvina Hall (1865)

I hear the Savior say,

"Thy strength indeed is small

Child of weakness,

watch and pray

Find in Me thine all in all"

Jesus paid it all,

All to Him I owe

Sin had left a crimson stain,

He washed it white as snow.

Come Thou Fount of Every Blessing

Robert Robison (1757)

Come, Thou Fount of every blessing

Tune my heart to sing Thy grace

Streams of mercy, never ceasing

Call for songs of loudest praise.

At the Cross
Isaac Watts (1707)

At the cross,

at the cross where I first saw the light

And the burden of my heart rolled away

It was there by faith I received my sight

And now I am happy all the day!

What a Friend We Have in Jesus

Joseph M. Scriven (1855)

What a friend we have in Jesus,

all our sins and griefs to bear!

What a privilege to carry

everything to God in prayer!

O what peace we often forfeit,

O what needless pain we bear

All because we do not carry

everything to God in prayer.

Turn Your Eyes Upon Jesus

Helen Lemmel (1922)

Turn your eyes upon Jesus

Look full in

His wonderful face

And the things of earth

will grow strangely dim

In the light of

His glory and grace.